DOGS AT WORK

THERAPY DOGS

BY MATT LILLEY

WWW.APEXEDITIONS.COM

Copyright © 2023 by Apex Editions, Mendota Heights, MN 55120. All rights reserved. No part of this book may be reproduced or utilized in any form or by any means without written permission from the publisher.

Apex is distributed by North Star Editions:
sales@northstareditions.com | 888-417-0195

Produced for Apex by Red Line Editorial.

Photographs ©: Shutterstock Images, cover, 1, 4–5, 6–7, 10–11, 12, 13, 14–15, 18–19, 20, 21, 22–23, 24–25, 26, 27; iStockphoto, 9, 16–17, 29

Library of Congress Control Number: 2022912279

ISBN
978-1-63738-428-2 (hardcover)
978-1-63738-455-8 (paperback)
978-1-63738-508-1 (ebook pdf)
978-1-63738-482-4 (hosted ebook)

Printed in the United States of America
Mankato, MN
012023

NOTE TO PARENTS AND EDUCATORS

Apex books are designed to build literacy skills in striving readers. Exciting, high-interest content attracts and holds readers' attention. The text is carefully leveled to allow students to achieve success quickly. Additional features, such as bolded glossary words for difficult terms, help build comprehension.

TABLE OF CONTENTS

CHAPTER 1
AT THE HOSPITAL 4

CHAPTER 2
WHAT THERAPY DOGS DO 10

CHAPTER 3
WHERE DOGS CAN HELP 16

CHAPTER 4
TRAINING 22

COMPREHENSION QUESTIONS • 28
GLOSSARY • 30
TO LEARN MORE • 31
ABOUT THE AUTHOR • 31
INDEX • 32

CHAPTER 1

AT THE HOSPITAL

Finn is training to be a **therapy** dog. He and his **handler** visit patients at a hospital. Many dogs would be nervous. But Finn stays calm.

Therapy dogs learn to stay calm around new people and places.

An elderly woman is in one room. She is too weak to sit up. Finn lays his head next to her. She scratches his ears. She smiles.

A good therapy dog likes being petted.

FAST FACT
Therapy dogs often visit people for 10 to 15 minutes.

In another room, a boy is waiting to have **surgery**. Finn plays with the boy. Finn chases a ball. He helps the boy feel less worried.

KEEPING CLEAN

Therapy dogs get baths before they visit hospitals. That way, they won't make people sick by bringing in germs. Patients also wash their hands after dogs visit them.

Playing with animals can help patients feel less afraid.

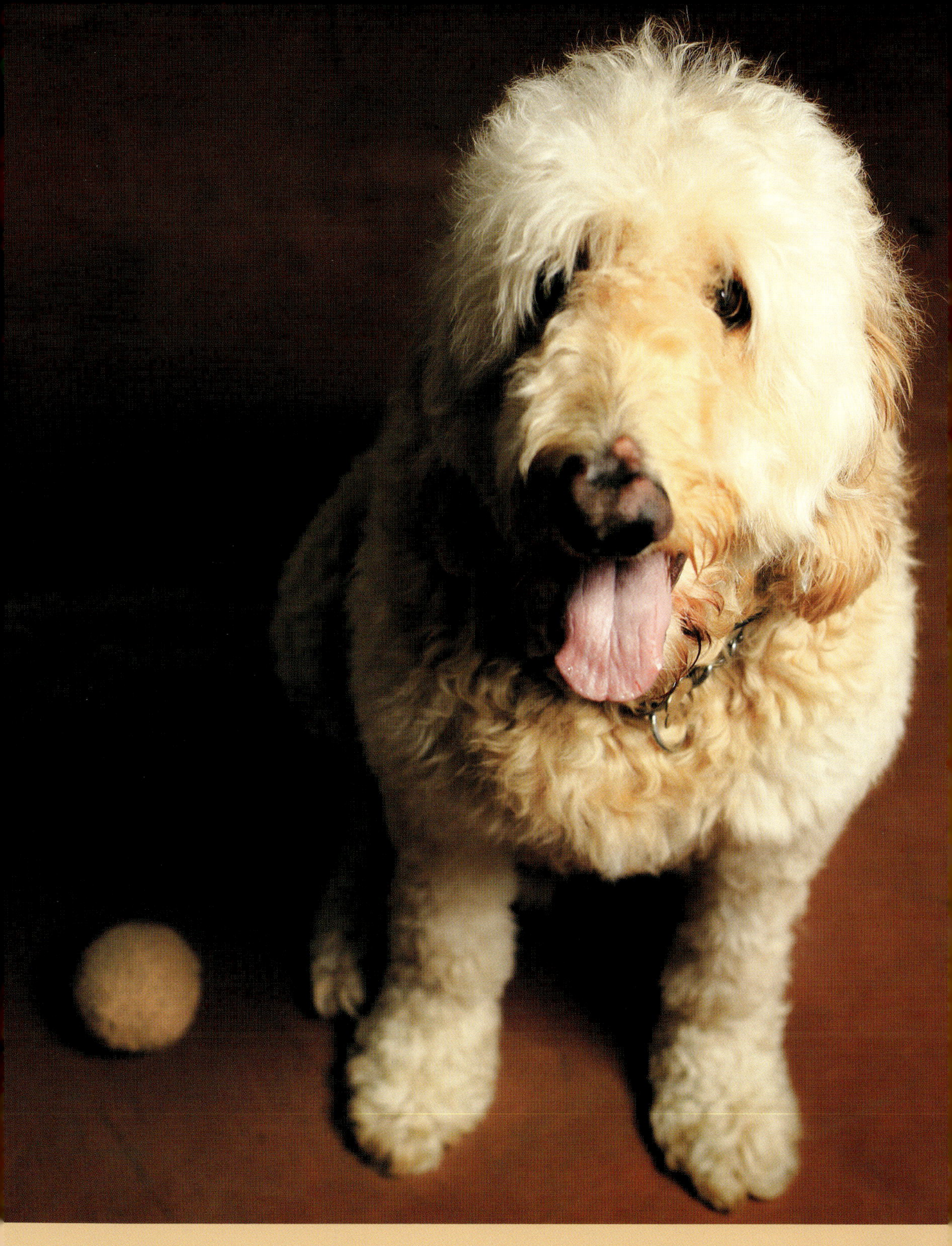

CHAPTER 2

WHAT THERAPY DOGS DO

Therapy dogs help people facing pain or problems. People spend time with the dogs. People cuddle or pet them.

Therapy dogs often help calm people's emotions.

FAST FACT

Dogs are just one type of therapy animal. Cats, rabbits, and guinea pigs can do this work, too.

BUBBLES
VOLUNTEER

Some patients find it easier to talk when animals are near.

Being near dogs helps many people feel less sad or **stressed**. Dogs can even help people feel less pain.

◀ Dogs help distract people from their problems. They give people something else to think about.

Each therapy dog has a handler. This person trains the dog. The handler helps people **interact** with the dog. The handler also helps keep the dog safe.

NOT SERVICE DOGS

Therapy dogs are not the same as service dogs. Service dogs are trained to help people with **disabilities** do tasks. Therapy dogs provide comfort and support.

Many handlers are volunteers. They don't get paid for their work.

CHAPTER 3

WHERE DOGS CAN HELP

Some therapy dogs work in schools and libraries. These dogs listen while kids read. Kids can be nervous about making mistakes. But dogs help them stay calm.

Reading out loud to dogs can help children learn.

Therapy dogs at nursing homes help older people feel less lonely.

Therapy dogs also work at nursing homes and hospitals. The dogs visit people who are sick or hurt. Seeing the dogs can cheer people up.

FAST FACT
Most therapy dogs live at home with their handlers.

After getting hurt or having surgery, patients may need help walking.

Dogs can even help people recover. After sickness or surgery, patients may need to walk or do **exercises**. Dogs can do these activities with them.

CAREFUL PLAY

Playing with dogs can help patients build strength. For example, games like fetch or tug-of-war can help people get exercise. Dogs must be careful not to play too roughly.

Playing tug-of-war with a dog can help patients get stronger.

CHAPTER 4

TRAINING

To become therapy animals, dogs must pass two tests. The first test focuses on obedience. Dogs learn commands such as "sit," "stay," and "heel."

Therapy dogs must learn to obey at least 10 commands.

Dogs also learn good manners. For example, they must not jump up on people.

IMPORTANT TRAITS

Therapy dogs can be any size or breed. But all therapy dogs must have certain traits. Dogs need to be friendly and calm. They must be gentle, too.

Patients may be weak or in pain. Therapy dogs must be careful not to hurt them.

For the second test, dogs must stay calm and focused around different people and sounds. If a dog passes both tests, it is officially **certified**.

Therapy dogs often wear vests when they are working.

Hospitals have many sounds and machines. Tests make sure dogs won't be scared of them.

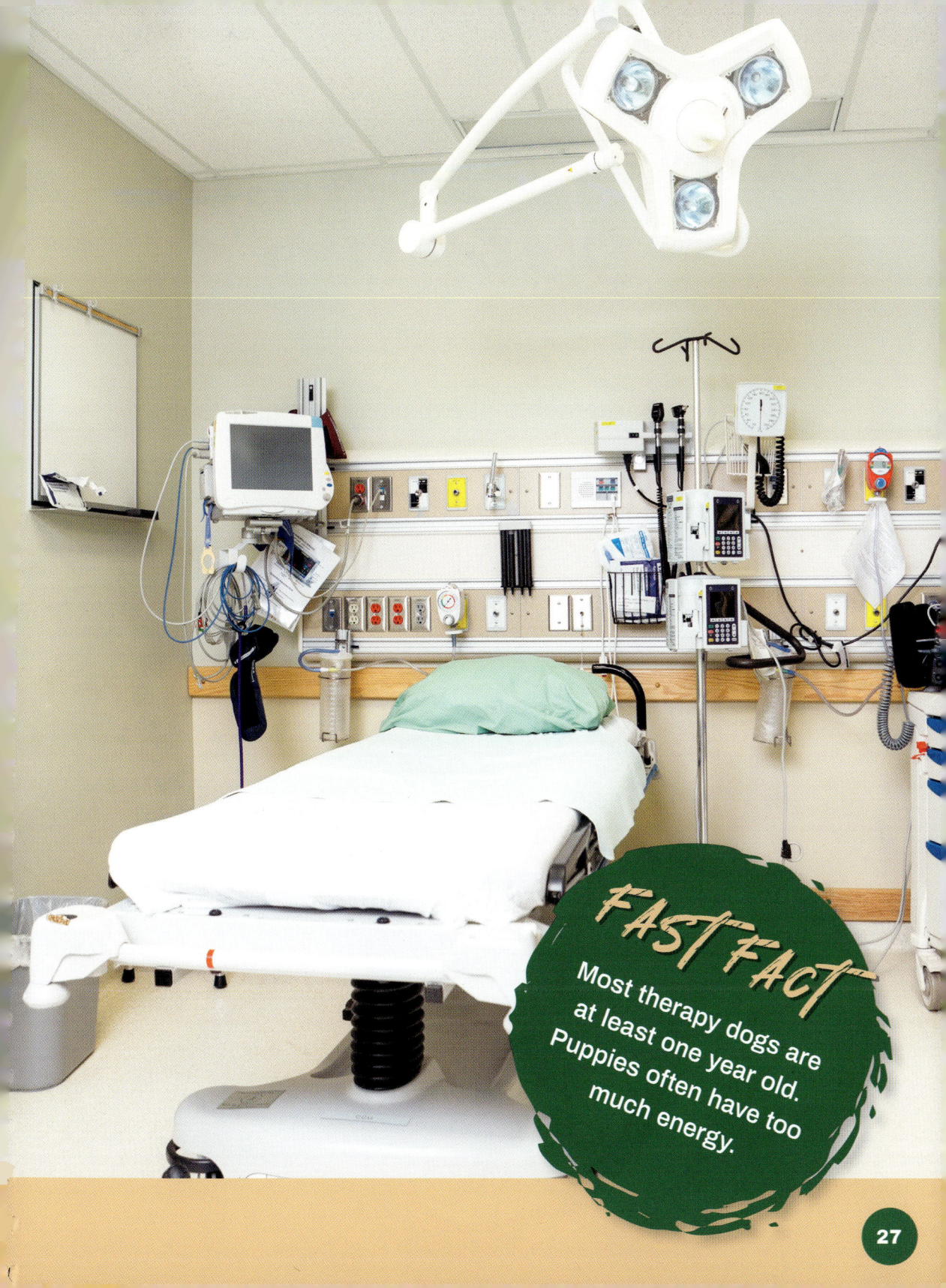

FAST FACT
Most therapy dogs are at least one year old. Puppies often have too much energy.

27

COMPREHENSION QUESTIONS

Write your answers on a separate piece of paper.

1. Write a paragraph that explains the main ideas of Chapter 2.

2. If you were in the hospital, would you want a visit from a therapy dog? Why or why not?

3. Which type of test must therapy dogs pass first?
    - A. a reading test
    - B. an obedience test
    - C. a test to stay calm and focused

4. Why is it important for therapy dogs to stay focused?
    - A. They must stay away from people.
    - B. They must not listen to their handlers.
    - C. They must obey their handlers in many places.

5. What does **recover** mean in this book?

Dogs can even help people recover. After sickness or surgery, patients may need to walk or do exercises.

    A. get hurt
    B. stay sick
    C. get better

6. What does **manners** mean in this book?

Dogs also learn good manners. For example, they must not jump up on people.

    A. correct ways to spell words
    B. correct ways to act around others
    C. correct ways to eat food

Answer key on page 32.

GLOSSARY

breed
A specific type of dog that has its own look and abilities.

certified
Proved to have certain skills and training, often by passing a test.

disabilities
Limits or differences in a person's senses or movement.

exercises
Movements that people do to get stronger.

handler
A person who works with and trains an animal.

interact
To talk or do things with others.

stressed
Tense, angry, or afraid because of a problem.

surgery
When doctors make cuts in the body to solve problems.

therapy
Treatment that helps with healing.

TO LEARN MORE

BOOKS

Davidson, B. Keith. *Service Dog.* New York: Crabtree Branches, 2022.

Laughlin, Kara L. *Therapy Dogs.* New York: AV2 by Weigl, 2019.

Pearson, Marie. *Dog Trainer.* North Mankato, MN: Capstone Press, 2019.

ONLINE RESOURCES

Visit **www.apexeditions.com** to find links and resources related to this title.

ABOUT THE AUTHOR

Matt Lilley has an MS in scientific and technical writing. The focus of his degree was on medical writing for kids. He loves researching and writing about all sorts of topics. He lives in Minnesota with his family.

INDEX

C
calm, 4, 16, 24, 26
commands, 22

E
exercises, 20–21

H
handler, 4, 14, 19
hospitals, 4, 8, 19

L
libraries, 16

N
nursing homes, 19

P
patients, 4, 8, 20–21
playing, 8, 21

R
reading, 16
recover, 20

S
schools, 16
service dogs, 14
sickness, 8, 19–20
surgery, 8, 20

T
tests, 22, 26
training, 4, 14

V
visits, 4, 7–8, 19

ANSWER KEY:
1. Answers will vary; 2. Answers will vary; 3. B; 4. C; 5. C; 6. B